THE STORY BEHIND
APRIL FOOLS' DAY

MELISSA RAÉ SHOFNER

PowerKiDS press™

New York

Published in 2020 by The Rosen Publishing Group, Inc.
29 East 21st Street, New York, NY 10010

First Edition

Editor: Tanya Dellaccio
Book Design: Reann Nye

Photo Credits: Cover, p.1 Diana Haronis dianasphotoart.com/Moment Open/Getty Images; pp. (background) 4, 6, 8, 10, 12, 14, 16, 18, 20, 22 Preto Perola/Shutterstock.com; p. 5 PeopleImages/Getty Images; p. 7 https://commons.wikimedia.org/wiki/File:Fran%C3%A7ois_Clouet_004.jpg; p. 9 Gustavo Frazao/ Shutterstock.com; p. 11 Africa Studio/Shutterstock.com; p. 13 BABAROGA/Shutterstock.com; p. 15 StanislavBeloglazov/Shutterstock.com; p. 17 makarenko7/Shutterstock.com; p. 19 DEA/G. DAGLI ORTI/De Agostini/Getty Images; p. 21 Universal History Archive/ Universal Images Group/Getty Images; p. 22 susan.k./ Moment Open/Getty Images.

Library of Congress Cataloging-in-Publication Data

Names: Shofner, Melissa Raé, author.
Title: The story behind April Fools' Day / Melissa Raé Shofner.
Description: New York : PowerKids Press, [2020] | Series: Holiday Histories |
  Includes webography. | Includes index.
Identifiers: LCCN 2018048737| ISBN 9781725300323 (paperback) | ISBN
  9781725300347 (library bound) | ISBN 9781725300330 (6 pack)
Subjects: LCSH: April Fools' Day–Juvenile literature. | April Fools'
  Day–History.
Classification: LCC GT4995.A6 S36 2020 | DDC 394.262–dc23
LC record available at https://lccn.loc.gov/2018048737

Manufactured in the United States of America

CPSIA Compliance Information: Batch #CSPK19. For Further Information contact Rosen Publishing, New York, New York at 1-800-237-9932.

CONTENTS

Mystery History

April Fools' Day is **celebrated** each year on April 1. No one knows how the holiday got its start. People around the world play tricks on each other. Be on the lookout for salt in the sugar bowl or a toy spider in your shoe!

Old Origins

People have celebrated April Fools' Day for hundreds of years. Some people think it started in France in the mid-16th century. Around this time, King Charles IX decided that the new year would start on January 1 instead of the first day of spring.

Some people continued to follow the old idea that the new year started in late March or early April, when spring began. Others called these people fools. They sometimes tricked the "fools" into thinking the wrong thing.

1

APRIL
FOOLS'
DAY

8

Watch Your Back!

When people in France play tricks on each other, the person who's tricked is called an "April fish." You can often see people walking around with paper fish taped to their backs on April Fools' Day in this country!

Happy Hilaria

The **ancient** Romans celebrated Hilaria on March 25. Hilaria was a lot like April Fools' Day. Hilaria was a fun-filled **festival** with parades and jokes to celebrate the end of winter. Is this how the holiday began? We may never know!

13

Other Fun Festivals

April Fools' Day is like several other holidays around the world. On Holi, the **Hindu** festival of colors, people throw colored **powder** at each other and play jokes. Some people think today's April Fools' Day celebrations may have been shaped by Holi celebrations.

During Purim, a Jewish festival, people wear **costumes**, play jokes on each other, and throw big parties. Sizdah Bedar is the Persian New Year. Families laugh and play to remove bad thoughts from their minds. These holidays are celebrated in early spring, too.

Purim festival

Feast of Fools

In **medieval** England and France, the Catholic Church held a celebration called the Feast of Fools. It took place in early January, but some people think it led to April Fools' Day. During the Feast of Fools, people threw big parties and wore costumes.

Church leaders thought it was good for everyone to have a bit of fun on this holiday. The Feast of Fools was banned in the 1400s when it got too wild. However, people continued to celebrate it for hundreds of years.

21

Foolish Fun

People have been playing tricks on each other for hundreds of years, but we might never know for sure how April Fools' Day got its start. Remember that jokes should never harm others. April Fools' Day is about being silly and having fun!

GLOSSARY

ancient: Of, coming from, or belonging to a time that was long ago in the past.

celebrate: To do something special or enjoyable for an important event or holiday.

costume: The clothes that are worn by someone who is trying to look like a different person or thing.

festival: A special time or event when people gather to celebrate something.

Hindu: Relating to Hinduism, a major religion of south Asia.

medieval: Of or relating to the Middle Ages, the period of European history from about AD 500 to about 1500.

powder: A dry substance made up of tiny pieces of something.

INDEX

WEBSITES

Due to the changing nature of Internet links, PowerKids Press has developed an online list of websites related to the subject of this book. This site is updated regularly. Please use this link to access the list: www.powerkidslinks.com/HH/april